A CLEAN CITY:
THE GREEN CONSTRUCTION STORY

Robyn C. Friend
and
Judith Love Cohen

Edited by Lee Rathbone

Cascade
Pass, Inc.

www.CascadePass.com

Copyright © 2008 by Cascade Pass, Inc.
Published by Cascade Pass, Inc.
4223 Glencoe Avenue, Suite C-105
Marina del Rey, CA 90292-8801
Phone: (310) 305-0210
Web Site: http://www.CascadePass.com
Printed in China by South China Printing Co. Ltd

A Clean City: The Green Construction Story was written by Robyn C. Friend and Judith Love Cohen, and edited by Lee Rathbone. Book design by David Katz, and graphic design by Kana Tatekawa of Momo Communications, Inc. and Ashley Whipple of DPR Construction, Inc.

This book is one of a series that emphasizes the environment and the value of preserving it by depicting people and organizations who are working to meet the challenges.

Other books in the series include:
A Clean Sky: The Global Warming Story
A Clean Sea: The Rachel Carson Story

Library of Congress Cataloging-in-Publication Data

Friend, Robyn C., 1955-
    A clean city : the green construction story / Robyn C. Friend and Judith Love Cohen ; edited by Lee Rathbone. – 1st ed.
    p. cm.
    ISBN 1-880599-85-6 (hard cover) – ISBN 1-880599-84-8 (pbk.)
    1. Sustainable buildings–Design and construction–Juvenile literature. 2. Sustainable architecture–Juvenile literature. 3. Building–Environmental aspects–Juvenile literature. I. Cohen, Judith Love, 1933- II. Rathbone, Lee. III. Title.
TH880.F75 2008
720'.47–dc22
        2008012172

Introduction

A Clean City: The Green Construction Story by Robyn C. Friend and Judith Love Cohen tells us the little-known story of how architects, engineers and builders have been working hard for decades to consider the impact the construction of a building has on the environment and what sustainable choices are available to them. *Green Buildings* are less harmful to the environment because they save energy, reuse valuable resources, improve air quality and recycle materials so that future generations will enjoy the Earth as we know it today.

If someone mentions the word "building" to you, what comes into your mind? Maybe you think of "the three little pigs." One of them built a house of straw, one built a house of twigs, and one built a house of bricks. Or, maybe you think of a beaver who builds dams out of sticks, gravel and mud.

You might think about people you learned about in your classes: Eskimos who build igloos of ice and snow, people in the tropics who build huts of palm leaves, desert people who build houses of adobe blocks, the Egyptians who built pyramids of stone, or Greeks who built temples of marble.

Until a hundred years ago or so, people in America still mostly built simple buildings from the materials they could get easily. The California missions were built of sun-dried clay bricks that kept the insides of the buildings cool in the summer and warm in the winter. In the very warm and humid parts of America, people learned to bake clay bricks in an oven to make a ceramic finish to help cool the inside of the building, and to use shutters and shadings to reduce the heat from sunshine while allowing air and light to go inside.

Invented centuries ago, an igloo has the potential to be up to **40 DEGREES WARMER** inside than outside. The snow and ice help trap body heat inside, and the walls help block the cold wind.

But technologies over the last hundred years have stopped using this kind of simplicity. They have become more complicated and energy dependent. In our modern cities, we build sealed-up buildings with windows that don't open for fresh air and with no way to get natural sunlight inside. Air-conditioning and heating systems, artificial light, and separate cubicles to work in are included in our new buildings. These buildings take a lot of work and materials to build, but even more important, it takes a lot of work and energy to keep them functional, year after year.

These buildings don't use the natural cooling and heating cycles of night and day, they don't use the natural breezes to give us air movement, they don't use the sunlight to read by, and when things wear out, we just throw them in the trash and buy replacements. A lot of materials and energy are being wasted.

Every year people fill enough garbage trucks to form a line that would stretch from the earth, halfway to the moon.

Source: Clean Air Council

But a few years ago, architects, engineers and builders began to think differently about how buildings are being designed, constructed and used. They started to consider our planet's resources, thinking about something called *sustainability*.

If people continue to use more resources and materials, such as water, food, wood, and vegetables in a year than the Earth is able to produce, then we eventually will run out of natural resources. So we need to focus on ways to use less!

Some sustainable ways to build buildings are all simple common sense methods:

- Build buildings with windows that open, outdoor spaces and rooftop gardens.
- Build homes and businesses close together.
- Reuse and recycle all building materials and equipment.

There are many different options.

So how has this idea of sustainability in constructing buildings been received?

A lot has changed in the past 10 years. A new building today is built by a project team consisting of the owner, the architect or designer, the engineer, and a builder/contractor.

The owner is the person who will use the finished building, and who therefore sets goals for the project team. Goals can include how much it will cost, when it will be finished and what environmentally friendly materials should be used. The design and construction professionals can then figure out the best ways to meet those goals.

For example, by using sustainability principles, the energy saved over the lifetime of the building will often pay for any extra costs for building green. In fact, the position of a building on the site can save energy. Depending upon the region, a building facing east/west will be exposed to more direct sunlight and be warmer than those facing north/south.

How does green building happen?

The process begins when the owner decides to build a new building or project.

Using a lot of glass and windows allows the sun in to light the building naturally, without using electricity.

Let's follow an owner, Joe, as he plans to build an office building. Joe wants to use sustainable principles, and he knows he needs help to build green. He needs to find an architect, an engineer and a builder, who are all experienced in sustainable design and construction. After a careful search, Joe has decided to hire Janet to be the architect. Janet knows the right engineers and builders and suggests several that have experience in green building and are willing to work as a team. Soon, Joe and Janet have hired Jennifer, the engineer, and Bob, the general contractor, to work with them on planning the project and how to best achieve Joe's goals.

The first decision is where to build. Joe was thinking about a beautiful, quiet, countryside area that has never been built on, called a *greenfield*. But Janet, Jennifer and Bob suggest a more "green" choice: build in a city area, where there is already a building. That way the greenfield can remain quiet and natural, and the owner can make use of the existing roads and utilities, like running water and electricity, that are already on the site. Joe and his employees also can save on fuel costs, since a city building will likely be near other places they will need to go, like supermarkets, schools, the post office, and the library. It also might be near bus stops and subway stations, so Joe's employees can get to work without driving a car.

GOAL	STEPS	EXAMPLES	RESULTS
Environment	Select building site 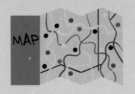	Build on a city lot rather than on a "Greenfield" country area	Preserves existing wild space, reuses an abandoned or previously used urban lot
Social	Lots of natural light Adjustable personal temperatures Windows that open Courtyards	Sunshades, Windows 	Improves "mood" and productivity 
Environment	Use new building materials made from recycled materials	Tile, Carpet	Less debris goes to landfill, lower use of natural resources
Environment	Use rapidly renewable materials	Use bamboo or cork	Reduces impacts on forests
Environment	Reuse old or salvaged materials 	Reuse window and door frames. Reuse large wooden beams and boards. Use old materials as decorative or structural elements. Save trees and shrubs from the site to plant as landscaping around the building.	Less debris goes to landfill, lower use of natural resources 

When a suitable location has been found, the team has to consider if the building that already exists on the site should be torn down or remodeled. Joe decides that he needs a different kind of building than the one that is there, plus the existing building is very old and no longer meets current building codes or rules. So the team starts to plan what the new building will be like, and how it will be used. The charts on pages 11, 13, and 15 show some of the choices and how they will relate to Joe's goals.

Will it be a single building that covers the entire site? Or will it be several buildings around a courtyard, so the workers can have a nice place outdoors to eat their lunches or take a break?

What materials will be used to build the building? Wood, steel, concrete? How much will be reused from other buildings, and how much can be reused from the building they will tear down to build the new one?

How much of the building materials will be new, and how much of the new materials will be from easily renewable sources, like bamboo?

How much of the materials will be from recycled, recyclable, or reusable materials?

GREEN BUILDING OPTIONS

GOAL	STEPS	EXAMPLES	RESULTS
Environment	Dispose of waste materials properly	Debris from construction and deconstruction recycled or reused	Less debris goes to landfill, lower use of natural resources
Economic	Save energy used in air-conditioning	Air circulation and modification in raised flooring	Less energy used in modifying temperatures for comfort
Economic	Save energy used in heating	Window placement and light shelves for passive solar heating	
Economic	Save energy used in cooling	Window shades for maintaining cool interior temperatures	
Economic	Save energy used in cooling	"Night Sky" water cooling	
Social	Low toxicity	Low VOC paints, glues and sealants	Builders and building occupants breathe fewer toxins

And what about energy? Maybe they could use the sun for lighting, heating and making electricity or maybe they could harness energy from the wind, much like the old-fashioned windmills used to grind wheat. Some of the energy systems used may cost Joe more money in the building, but they will save a lot more later in the lower energy demand needed to heat, cool or light up the building. Bob, Jennifer and Janet will use computer programs to help Joe figure out the costs of different ideas. They also need to decide where the new building should be located on the site, how best to make use of the shade and the sun on the site, and how the building will be heated in the winter and cooled in the summer.

The team also will look at plumbing fixtures, such as toilets that use less water, and other items on the Green Building Options Chart.

GREEN BUILDING OPTIONS

GOAL	STEPS	EXAMPLES	RESULTS
Economic	Use roof insulation to save energy	"Green" roof	Maintain comfortable temperatures inside the building
Environment	Use roof insulation to reduce water going to sewer systems		Absorbs rainwater so there is less water and cleaner water going into the sewer system and out to the ocean
Social	Use roof insulation to absorb sunlight		Absorbs sunlight so less light is reflected back out, heating local air
Economic	Use wind for cooling	Cool tower	Less energy used in modifying temperatures for comfort
Social	Use wind for cooling		No coolants released into atmosphere
Environment	Low water use	Low-flow plumbing fixtures	Less water used
Environment	Reduce water use	Low-water landscaping	

While the design details are being finalized, the construction details are being planned. How will the existing building be torn down (deconstructed) and how will the new building be built? Bob has a lot of experience in removing leftover materials from a deconstruction project, and has good ways to make sure the building materials with value do not end up in the landfill. He also has good ideas for how to reuse some of the existing structural elements and materials so they won't go to waste.

We've described an imaginary project built by our imaginary owner, Joe, with his architect, Janet, the engineer, Jennifer, and the builder, Bob. Now, let's look at some of the green choices that real building teams can make, and how they were used in real building projects.

Pieces of metal from an old building can be recycled and reformed into cars, nuts and bolts, and other metal products.

17

The first sustainable building idea is the *night-sky cooling system*. This means to cool water using the dark of night, then using that chilled water in the daytime to cool the building. Water is sprayed over the roof to chill under the cold night sky. Then the water is collected and stored in a large tank and pumped through pipes in the floor of the building during the day. This uses much less energy and water than conventional cooling systems, and no chemicals at all, just water.

The Global Ecology Center for the Carnegie Institution of Washington, located at Stanford University, is an office for research and environmental science. They wanted to make a building that would be energy-efficient, use mostly sustainable materials, and be comfortable and safe for the people who would work in it.

In addition to the *night-sky cooling system*, they also have a *cool tower*. Instead of air-conditioning, the cool tower uses a steel *wind catcher* to capture natural breezes that pass over the building. As the captured air moves through the tower, it is sprayed with a mist of water that cools the air even more before it enters the building's lobby. It's just like a cool breeze.

COOLING TOWER

WARM AIR   85° F

COOL AIR
59° F

CARNEGIE INSTITUTION
OF WASHINGTON
GLOBAL ECOLOGY CENTER

Some green ideas are used to make people feel more comfortable in their living and working spaces. Having buildings around an open *courtyard*, and lots of windows (*daylighting*) to let in light and fresh air helps make workers more comfortable and productive. People like to be able to see the outdoors even when they have to be inside.

Aspect Communications is a provider of software and services to help other companies communicate. They wanted to build a healthy, environmentally sensitive workplace for their employees. The project team planned and built two, three-story buildings around a central courtyard. The courtyard includes ponds, fountains, and local plants and grasses that need only a little water, creating a natural environment for relaxing at work.

A two-story, open bridge connects the two buildings. The buildings also include a lot of windows that open for fresh air and natural daylighting. The third floors of the buildings feature high ceilings and special windows called *clerestory windows* that allow people to see the sky and feel more connected to the outdoors.

Drawings like this one are called renderings. They are illustrations that architects use to plan out the way a building will look.

ASPECT COMMUNICATIONS

A *bioswale* is a man-made drainage channel that keeps rainwater and irrigation runoff away from local rivers and oceans. The bioswale removes silt and pollution from the runoff water by filtering the water through plants, compost, or other hard materials like river stones. It is especially useful around parking lots, where pollutants from cars would otherwise run off into the sewer and quickly to our oceans, rivers, and lakes without any filtration.

Roche Molecular Diagnostics, in Pleasanton, CA, built a new three-story research building. The building includes bioswales to channel rainwater. Some of the other sustainable features include a *white roof membrane* that keeps the building cool by reflecting rather than absorbing sunlight, which makes the building warmer and requires additional cooling. The white roof also lasts longer than a conventional roof system.

BIOSWALE

23

WATER
with pollutants from
roads and buildings

STONES

SOIL

SAND

FILTERED WATER REENTERS
THE GROUND WATER SUPPLY

ROCHE MOLECULAR DIAGNOSTICS

Let's look at a *green roof*. That doesn't mean a roof that is colored green, but a roof that has plants growing on it! Why is this a good idea? A wood or tile roof allows rainwater to flow off the roof and into the sewer system and then to streams and rivers and eventually out into the ocean without any filtration of harmful substances. A green roof absorbs most of the water, which is filtered through the soil just like the bioswales, so the runoff water is filtered and much cleaner.

A green roof absorbs sunlight, using the warmth of the sun to help plants on the roof grow, instead of heating up the house or the neighborhood. A green roof also provides better *insulation*, meaning that the building stays warmer in winter, and cooler in summer. Some green roofs also reflect the sun to keep buildings cooler.

The National Audio Visual Conservation Center for the Library of Congress in Virginia houses one of the largest movie and music collections in the world. It has a 5.5-acre green roof, one of the largest green roofs of its kind on the East Coast. The roof is used for outdoor space and, more importantly, helps reduce the temperature of the surrounding spaces.

ABSORBING

REFLECTING

INSULATING

25

NATIONAL AUDIO VISUAL CONSERVATION CENTER

An important part of green building is *reusing* materials, either from other buildings, called salvaging, or items made from *recycled* materials.

Intuit, Inc. is a company that makes software. They wanted to bring their employees from several locations around the city of San Diego into one single location. Rather than building a new structure on a greenfield, they decided on a property that already had four buildings on it, and then remodeled them to meet their goals of sustainability, low impact, and green maintenance.

For the Intuit project, the team used carpet with a high percentage of *recycled* materials and bamboo paneling. They also paid a lot of attention to the construction waste from the job site and made sure that only a minimum, less than 30%, of the construction materials ended up in the landfill. One idea that helped achieve this was to work with local suppliers to deliver materials in packaging that could be reused rather than thrown away.

Another company, VMware, a maker of software that runs a virtual computer inside of a real computer, used reclaimed hardwood flooring saved from a Wisconsin barn once owned by Thomas Edison for their campus in Palo Alto, CA.

Be a part of the solution. How you can help!

While you probably will have a few more years of school before you can build your own building, you can:

1. *Plant wild grasses or even a native tree. Native plants save water.*

2. *Take shorter showers, don't leave the water running, do only full loads of laundry and dishes, turn off the water when you brush your teeth. Efficient water use saves water.*

3. *Open a window when the weather allows, don't use the heat if you can put on a sweater. Natural ventilation uses less energy.*

4. *Think about giving things away rather than throwing them out. Buy used items at places like garage sales or thrift stores. Salvaged materials reduce the waste going to landfills.*

PLANT WILD GRASSES

TAKE SHORTER SHOWERS

OPEN A WINDOW

YARD SALE

DON'T THROW THINGS AWAY

5. *Move your sunshade to allow light in when you need it and keep the sun out when you don't. Sunshades save energy.*

6. *Turn off the lights when you leave a room. Lighting controls reduce energy use and heat gain.*

7. *Open windows at night to cool down interior, so less air-conditioning will be used. Night cooling during summer nights can save energy on air-conditioning.*

While architects, engineers and builders can do a lot of the things we've listed, you can play a part, and if you keep the goals in mind, you will select better designed and built things as you make more of your own decisions.

A very special way for you to help is to become an architect or an engineer or a builder. **WHAT CAN *YOU* DO?**

Do you like to paint and draw? Do you like playing with colors and fabrics? You could be an interior designer, learn about interior materials made from recycled, recyclable or reusable materials, or materials made from rapidly renewable resources, like bamboo!

Do you like plants and gardens? You could become a landscape designer who specializes in drought-tolerant landscaping. Or you could specialize in designing green roofs!

Do you like playing with Legos or building forts? You could become an architect, and learn to design green buildings or become a builder and learn to construct buildings using sustainable principles!

You could become a materials engineer, and discover new ways to make building materials from recycled, recyclable or reusable materials. You could become a civil engineer, and design green buildings, highways, and waterworks for your city, state, or national government. Or you could be a structural engineer, and design green buildings, towers, or stadiums.

FUN FACTS

Fun Fact 1:

Did you know that some of today's green building ideas have been used for thousands of years?

- The Romans heated their homes with pipes of hot water underneath their floors.

- The ancient Persians cooled their homes in summer with wind towers, called "badgir," which means wind catcher. The very tall towers captured breezes and funneled them into the rooms below, cooling the inside of the house.

- The ancient Persians also made ice! They built small buildings with very thick walls, called "yakhchal," which means ice house. All winter long, they stuffed snow into the yakhchal, packing it in very tight. All summer long, they could cut slabs of ice from the yakhchal!

- The Anasazi Indians of Colorado built their homes in the sides of canyons, using the natural overhang of the cliff face to shade the sun in the summertime, while allowing the sun to warm their homes in the wintertime.

Fun Fact 2:

Did you know that buildings can be made of straw bales, clay, mud, and old tires?

Fun Fact 3:

Do you know what biomimicry is?

It's when people study the ways that animals and plants solve problems of survival and adapt those ways for use by humans. For example:

- An oyster creates its shell out of only the materials it has at hand (sand, water) and it is superior to any ceramic products that humans have been able to create!

- Ants in Africa create huge anthills with air circulation spaces that keep the interior within a temperature range that keeps the ants comfortable.

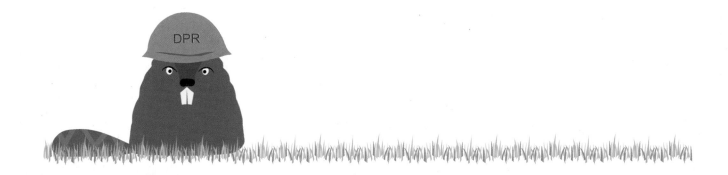

GLOSSARY

Biomass: Biomass refers to living and recently dead living material (like plants or animal waste) that can be used as fuel (Biofuel) or for industrial production. Plastics can be made from biomass. These plastics can be made more cheaply than petroleum-based plastics, and can dissolve in seawater.

Bioswale: A drainage channel built to filter runoff water from rain and irrigation before the water goes into the watershed or sewer system. The channel is lined with growing plants, compost, or rock. It filters out silt, pollutants, and bacteria.

Clerestory windows: In modern architecture these are windows above eye level that allow light into a space. They provide light into a building without using lower wall space for windows.

Construction debris: This is the leftover junk from demolishing or constructing a building. It can include torn up concrete, extra lumber, carpeting or wallboard, used shipping materials, broken glass, and lots of other stuff.

Cooling tower: A modern cooling tower is designed to catch the wind coming from any direction, and direct the cool air into the building, to keep its temperature cool without using electricity or pollutants.

Curtain wall: A curtain wall is the outside face of a building that does not carry any weight except its own. You can see curtain walls in many modern buildings where the exterior of the building is entirely glass.

Daylighting: This means placing windows in buildings to allow enough natural light into the interior of the building so that artificial light is not necessary.

Deconstruction: In the building industry, deconstruction means tearing down a building, in a careful way, to reuse building materials, and to make sure that surrounding people or buildings are not harmed.

Deforestation: This is when large areas of trees are cut down and not replanted. This can cause previously mature eco-systems to become wastelands.

Durability: This means that the materials referred to will last a very long time, or can be reusable.

Energy-efficient: This means using energy in a smarter way so that less overall energy can accomplish the same task. An energy-efficient home would, for example, have insulation so it would use less energy to maintain a comfortable temperature than the energy-wasteful home that has no insulation.

FSC certification: The Forest Stewardship Council (FSC) is an international non-profit organization established in 1993 to promote responsible management of the world's forests, to prevent their destruction. The FSC has established standards so that people can buy forest products like wood or paper that have been harvested in a more sustainable way.

Galvanized: This means that iron or steel has been coated with hot molten zinc to prevent corrosion.

Green roof: This is a roof that has plants growing on it. Special materials are used to make sure the roof is sealed against leaks, and then plants are planted on top of a soil layer. This keeps a lot of rainwater from flowing off the building, and keeps the sunlight's heat from reflecting off the roof.

Greenfield: This is an area of pristine nature, where there has never been any kind of building or development.

Habitat loss: This happens when areas are so disturbed by building or development that the plants or animals that live there can no longer thrive.

Landfill: When you throw things away, this is where it ends up. Your trash can stay here for decades or centuries without decaying into the soil.

LEED: Leadership in Energy and Environmental Design (LEED) is a Green Building Rating System, developed by the U.S. Green Building Council. It provides a set of standards for environmentally sustainable construction.

Light shelf: This is a projection on the outside of a window that reflects light upward onto the ceiling to inside and allows natural light to brighten the inside without adding heat.

Night sky radiant cooling: This is a way to cool a building during warm weather without using conventional air conditioning, which uses a lot of electricity and toxic chemicals. On hot nights, water is sprayed over the roof of the building so that the night air might cool it. The cooled water is collected in a tank. During the day, the cooled water is pumped through the building, cooling it.

Non-toxic: Materials like paint, carpeting and glue can give off fumes that are dangerous to health, and therefore toxic. Non-toxic materials are available that use less or no chemicals and reduce indoor and outdoor air pollution.

Reclaimed, Reused: This means carefully removed materials that can be used again in another place. For every million board feet of reclaimed lumber, 1,000 acres of forest are saved.

Recycled: This means that materials which have been designed and used for one purpose are processed for another purpose, taking old materials and making them into new products. Newspapers, for example, are recycled into a variety of products.

Salvage: This is the process of removing materials to be reused or recycled. Faucets or furniture removed from one building can be reused in another.

Skin: This is the outer layer of a building. It can be a curtain wall or a material like brick or stone.

Storm water management: When it rains, lots of water reaches the ground, collects, and flows downhill. Storm water management is a strategy to keep the rainwater from causing problems, such as overflowing storm drains, or houses slipping down a hill.

Sunshade: This keeps direct sunlight from getting inside a building where it would increase heat and cause glare.

Sustainability: Sustainability is using our earth's resources at a slower rate than nature can produce them so that they last longer and can be maintained at a certain level forever. For example, a sustainable forest is where trees are harvested and replanted instead of clear-cut and abandoned.

VOC: Volatile Organic Compounds (VOCs) are organic chemical compounds that vaporize and enter the air, such as methane. They come from paint thinners, paints, varnishes, and chemicals used for sealing and finishing walls. They contribute to poor health and are considered a factor in indoor air quality.

A CLEAN CITY: THE GREEN CONSTRUCTION STORY

LESSON PLAN 1: Designing a Green Building

PURPOSE: To gain an understanding of how a design team makes a building "green."

MATERIALS: Pen and paper, construction paper, scissors, glue.

PROCEDURES: Have the children close their eyes and visualize a building as it is now.

Have them draw a part of the building that they can imagine changing to be more green; have them make notes on what should be changed; e.g., more windows, solar panels, florescent lights, green roof, floor heating.

Have children use construction paper and create a green version of the building.

Have each child describe what they have constructed and how it is more green than what they started with.

CONCLUSIONS: How is your new building different from the building you started with?

What features and materials have you added to your building?

What does it feel like when you are inside the new building?

LESSON PLAN 2:

PURPOSE: To gain an understanding of reducing, recycling and reusing.

MATERIALS: Pads of paper, two trash bins filled with pictures of various construction debris: concrete pieces, wood beam ends, window panes, old carpeting, old furniture, packaging.

PROCEDURE: Have the children divide into two teams and give each one a trash bin filled with the pictures as described above.

Have them take out the pictures of the items, one by one and have one of the children be the note taker and write down what the object is.

Have the children discuss what can be done with each item and what can be done in the future to reduce the amount of waste.

Have each team present their reuse, reduce, recycle strategy to the class.

CONCLUSIONS: What can you do with each of the items?

Faucets or furniture can be reused by construction people on another building. Packaging materials can be recycled. Carpets and concrete can be processed for reuse.

What can you do to reduce the volume of trash in the first place?

Vendors can be asked to provide materials in reusable containers instead of disposable packaging, building materials can be purchased in the appropriate size so there is no trim waste.

What happens to any trash or waste that remains in the trash bins? Why is this a problem?

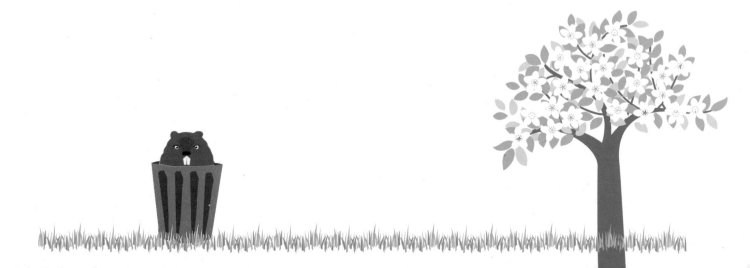

About the Contributors:

Christopher Gorthy, contributor, LEED®-Accredited Professional, is a preconstruction manager from DPR Construction, Inc. and a green guru for DPR's Falls Church, VA office, serving customers throughout the East Coast. Chris assists customers with green strategies, estimating and green construction projects. He also served as a member of the Washington D.C. Green Building task force, which helped set the standards and develop legislation that will improve the environment and quality of life for all District of Columbia workers and residents.

Matt Crandall, contributor, LEED®-Accredited Professional, is a project manager and green guru for DPR Construction, Inc. An active member of the U.S. Green Building Council's Northern California Chapter, Matt is involved in both LEED for Existing Buildings and LEED for New Construction projects and recently completed a green laboratory and research building for Roche Molecular Diagnostics in Pleasanton, CA. Matt has also played an integral role in helping DPR analyze its overall company carbon footprint and ways to reduce it.

Ted van der Linden, contributor, LEED®-Accredited Professional, is the director of sustainable construction for DPR Construction, Inc. An active member of the U.S. Green Building Council since 1998, Ted leads a group of green gurus across the country, helping to develop sustainable green building strategies and programs that move DPR toward one of its goals of having a "proven track record in being environmentally responsible in the way we do business." The Western Chapter Representative on the U.S. Green Building Council's national Board of Directors, Ted offers a range of expertise in all phases of commercial, industrial and sustainable construction.

Whitney Dorn, contributor, LEED®-Accredited Professional, is a project manager and green guru for DPR Construction, Inc., and has managed the building process for corporate offices, healthcare facilities, senior living facilities, biotech laboratories and pharmaceutical manufacturing for more than 15 years. She recently completed a new campus for Intuit, Inc., which is the largest LEED® for Commercial Interiors project built in San Diego county to date. An ACE Mentoring leader for Hoover High School, where she has taught more than 50 students about architecture, engineering and construction, she also has taught LEED courses at DPR for employees, subcontractors, architects and owners.

Ginny Dyson, contributor, LEED®-Accredited Professional, IIDA, is a senior associate and interior designer for DMJM ROTTET. In addition to projects for financial institutions, government and corporate facilities, Ginny has been an active member of the sustainable design community for many years, and since 2001 she has been an officer of the SMaRT Sustainable Product Standard Committee, an initiative of Market Transformation of Sustainability (MTS).

Kevin Burke, contributor, AIA, LEED®-Accredited Professional, is the director of practice for William McDonough + Partners. Named design partner in 2000, Kevin has worked closely with William McDonough to give form to WM+P's sustaining design principles over a broad array of project types and scales. His work encompasses a particular interest in the place-making through integrated design solutions.

Robyn C. Friend, author, is a singer, dancer, choreographer, and writer. She earned a Ph.D. in Iranian Linguistics at UCLA, and promptly launched a twenty-year career building spacecraft. She has written for both scholarly and popular publications on a wide variety of subjects, including folkloric dance, world music, linguistics, travel, and the exploration of Mars by balloon.

Judith Love Cohen, author, is a Registered Professional Electrical Engineer with bachelor's and master's degrees in engineering from the University of Southern California and University of California, Los Angeles. She has written plays, screenplays, and newspaper articles in addition to her series of children's books that began with You Can Be a Woman Engineer.

David Arthur Katz, art director, received his training in art education and holds a master's degree from the University of South Florida. He is a credentialed teacher in the Los Angeles Unified School District. His involvement in the arts has encompassed animation, illustration, and playwriting, poetry, and songwriting.

ACKNOWLEDGEMENTS

DPR Construction, Inc. is a national commercial general contractor specializing in technically challenging and sustainable projects. DPR would like to thank its project team members for helping to "build great things" on the following projects highlighted in this book:

ASPECT COMMUNICATIONS: Corporate Campus, San Jose, CA, **ARCHITECTS:** William McDonough + **Partners;** Form4 Architecture Inc., **CONSTRUCTION MANAGER:** Nova Partners

CARNEGIE INSTITUTION OF WASHINGTON: Global Ecology Center Research Building, Stanford, CA, **ARCHITECT:** EHDD Architecture

INTUIT INC.: Corporate Campus, San Diego, CA, **ARCHITECT:** Carrier-Johnson

PACKARD HUMANITIES INSTITUTE: National Audio Visual Conservation Center for the Library of Congress, Culpeper, VA, **ARCHITECTS:** SmithGroup; BAR Architects, OWNER'S PROJECT **MANAGER:** Faithful & Gould

ROCHE MOLECULAR DIAGNOSTICS: Research Building, Pleasanton, CA, **ARCHITECT:** DES Architects + Engineers, Inc.

VMWARE: Corporate Headquarters, Palo Alto, CA, **ARCHITECTS:** William McDonough + **Partners;** Form4 Architecture Inc.

Photography: Ed Asmuss Photography, Jeff Williams, John Ho Photography, Mert Carpenter Photography, Rien van Rijthoven, Sharon Risedorph Photography, Whittaker Photography, MastorakosPhotography.com.

DPR CONSTRUCTION SACRAMENTO OFFICE BUILDING

When completed in 2003, DPR's Sacramento office building was the first privately owned U.S. Green Building Council Leadership in Energy and Environmental Design (LEED®)-certified office building in the Sacramento Valley. The building also received the Governor's Environmental and Economic Leadership Award for sustainable facilities from California Governor Arnold Schwarzenegger. Some of the building's green features include:

- Wastewater systems, such as dual-flush toilets and low-flow showerheads that save approximately 175,000 gallons of water a year.

- A single-ply white roof that reflects the sun and absorbs very little heat to help minimize energy consumption, especially during the summer months when the average temperature reaches nearly 100 degrees.

- Recycled materials, including carpets, ceiling tiles, rubber flooring, glass, and bio-composite countertops made of compressed sunflower seed husks and newspaper.

In addition, DPR's offices in Falls Church, VA, Redwood City, CA, and San Francisco, CA, are all targeting LEED certification and feature green elements such as insulation made from old blue jeans, natural daylighting, and low-emitting materials , including paints, carpet and furniture adhesives. For more information, please visit DPR Construction's website at www.dprinc.com.